Whole Heart for Young Women

Feeling Good About Yourself

Amy L. Stark, Ph.D.

Copyright © 2017 Amy L. Stark, Ph.D.

All rights reserved.

ISBN: 1507549741
ISBN-13: 978-1507549742

CONTENTS

Acknowledgments   i

1. Deserving of Love   1
2. A Heart Hole   2
3. The Hole Grows   3
4. School & Sports   4
5. Alone with Yourself   5
6. A Journey   6
7. Learning to Love Yourself   7
8. Enjoying Life   8
9. The Amazing You   9
10. Discussion   10
11. Activities   16

ACKNOWLEDGMENTS

I want to thank all the children and teens I have worked with over the years. Through them, I have learned so much about where self-esteem issues start and the importance of addressing them early on. They have also taught me that self esteem is a journey not a destination. I also wish to thank my editor, Lisa Houser, for her guidance and assistance. And many thanks goes to Eileen Gaffen for getting my books out into the world.

1
DESERVING OF LOVE

"Give it your whole heart." That's what people say to encourage you to do your best. But what if your whole heart isn't whole? What if it has holes in it instead? In fact, what if there are holes where your feelings about you live? How can you give your "whole heart" then?

You were born and you were perfectly loveable. Not because you had all your fingers and toes, or your mother's eyes and your father's chin—but because you truly were a perfect, unique, human being. You didn't even have to DO anything to deserve love.

At that moment you deserved love just because you were you. And because you were born loveable, you can say "I am loveable" three times.

2
A HEART HOLE

You went home from the hospital and cried and ate and slept and grew. Sometimes you cried so hard that your parents couldn't calm you down. That's what babies do.

But sometimes the grown-ups grew tired or were in a hurry. Sometimes they got mad at other drivers or someone at the drive-through window. Sometimes they disagreed with each other. And while all that was happening around you, a tiny hole in the part of your heart that cares about you appeared.

3
THE HOLE GROWS

As you grew and went out into the world to discover what was there, you heard, "No!" or "That's enough of that" or "Why can't you listen to me?"

Because everyone makes mistakes, even grown-ups, you wondered if when you make a mistake if something was wrong with you. And the hole in the part of your heart that cares about you grew.

You grew bigger and went off to school and found that all the children in your class have holes, too. You knew they were there when you listened carefully to the things they said to each other. "You look like a hockey stick with hair," someone said to a skinny child. "Hey, Fatso," they shouted to an overweight girl. They even insult each other's families, "Your mother is sooooo ugly."

And you feel embarrassed and angry and hurt—as if no one likes you anymore. You must have done something wrong or the kids wouldn't be teasing you, right? You feel unlikeable, and even unlovable, sometimes.

And the hole grows.

4
SCHOOL & SPORTS

Teachers aren't all the same. Some teachers are supportive and build you up. They praise your efforts and applaud your improvements. Then the hole stays the same for a while—sometimes it even fills in a bit.

Sometimes teachers or grown-ups at the school have bad days, too. They might use a grouchy voice that hurts your feelings. When they tell you what you did wrong, you feel bad, like you can't ever seem to get anything right. And so the hole in the part of your heart that cares about you grows.

Some coaches are positive and they teach you to not give up but to practice. They notice when you try and when you improve. And the hole fills in a bit.

Other coaches scold you when you miss a shot or are not playing your best. They get angry at you and make you feel like you aren't good enough. And so the hole in the part of your heart that cares about you grows.

5
ALONE WITH YOURSELF

You try hard to be loved by fitting in. It's hard to stand up for yourself. Sometimes you " like " things on social media just so you won't be unfriended or blocked.

You may read mean comments about yourself or your friends on social media. Everyone knows about it at school and it really hurts. The hardest part is some people you thought were pretty nice don't stand up for you either. They seem to be going along with the comments. You feel like no one loves or understands you.

6

A JOURNEY

You have someone you are dating. They tell you that if you REALLY love them, you would send suggestive photos. You are desperate to be loved, so you send something. "It's ok," you say to yourself. "They will erase it after they view it and no one will see it."

But they don't. They screen shot it and send it around the school. Now, everyone knows. And the kids who know better and should stand up and say "no one deserves to be treated like this" say nothing. And you are alone.

You want to never leave the house again. It seems like there is no way out. Now everyone is looking at you and laughing.

Suddenly the hole in the part of your heart that cares about you is so big it is all you can see.

You feel like life is over.

7
LEARNING TO LOVE YOURSELF

Then, your very best friend says something to you. "Don't let this define you. You don't have to prove you are loveable. You are loveable".

"Wow," you think to yourself. When did my friend get so smart?

So, you do your homework—about yourself. You realize that everything you do, seems to be about proving that you are loveable.

If you have friends…it proves are you loveable. If you have someone to date, it proves you are loveable. If you do well at school, it proves you are loveable.

Then, you have an epiphany.

8
ENJOYING LIFE

If you already love yourself, you can focus on other things. You have friendships because you enjoy being with them. You date, because you enjoy someone's company and they enjoy yours. You do well in school because you enjoy your classes and love doing well.

You find meaning in what you do-and look for what you can be passionate about. How can you make a difference? What matters most to you?

Then, something happens. You actually like yourself. And, because you do, you find you can surround yourself with people you like, who like you back.

9
THE AMAZING YOU

And so the healing begins. At first you don't notice. The changes are so small. But with time and love and patience, the hole is filled. You become perfectly loveable, whole, and complete. Just as you were when you were born. And the place in your heart that cares about *you*, really does care about *you* again.

Since happily ever after does not come with a bigger house, a better job, a perfect body, or a fairy tale relationship, but rather from loving yourself, I am sure you will live happily ever after.

But, instead of the end, as in every other story, this is just THE BEGINNING... the beginning of a WHOLE new you, and the better life you have made possible for yourself.

10

DISCUSSION

1. When you are in a group of friends, how often do you check to make sure you have not left someone out? Why is that important?

Everyone knows what it feels like to be left out. It is very lonely. Remember that when you see someone sitting by themselves. Stand up and do something about it. If just a few people stand up, things change.

2. If your friends make fun of someone, how can you discuss how it must feel with them? Is there a way you could reach out for the person they are picking on?

Bullying of any kind, whether it's in person or not, is both damaging and painful. It's also very cowardly. Say something. If that does not work, tell someone about it. Just 'taking it' is not healthy and can cause you to have bad feelings.

If you see someone else getting picked on, say something about that. Change starts with you. No one should be bullied or cyber-bullied. Contact the school authorities and local police about it.

3. If a teacher is mean or bullies you, who could you tell? If they do it to someone else, what should you do?

Or if your boss is mean or bullies you, who could you tell? If they do it to someone else, what should you do?

Bosses should not berate you. You do have options. Don't just 'take it'. At school, contact someone in the counseling department for guidance or go directly to the principal. At a job, tell someone in human resources.

4. If you date someone and they are pushy or aggressive with you, what is the best way to handle it? What if they don't like you as much then?

If standing up for yourself bothers someone you date, they don't really like you - much less love you. You cannot be in any relationship based on changes either of you must make in order to be loveable. It will only get worse if you cannot be yourself. Get support and find something meaningful to do.

5. If someone you thought was a friend picks on other people, should you stop them? What if they start to do it to you?

If a friend picks on others, sooner or later they are going to pick on you. You are seeing a preview of coming attractions. Say something to your friend. Be honest. All relationships worth keeping are built on honesty.

6. How can you feel good about your looks without letting that be your primary focus?

There is a difference between looking your best because you enjoy how you feel when you do, versus doing what you do to be loveable.

You will find that if you try to lose weight, change your hair or get plastic surgery to be loveable, you will never be satisfied. All those things should be done because you want to change your look for you. Anything you do should be to be your best you…not so you can be loved. You are already loveable.

11
ACTIVITIES

1. Research the meaning of your name. Why were you given that name...ask your parents. Look up the meaning of your name.

2. Ask 5 people you know what they find special about you. Record their answers.

3. Write down your successes and accomplishments for the year. Leave room so that once a year you can enter the top 5 things. Do this for three years.

ABOUT THE AUTHOR

Dr. Amy Stark, Ph.D. is a highly respected clinical psychologist in the state of California. She received her doctorate in 1981 from the California School of Professional Psychology in San Diego, and her background in education is in child psychology.

Dr. Stark is best known for her work with high-conflict divorce situations. Dr. Stark brings her training in child psychology to her work with children of high-conflict divorce.

One of the unique techniques that Dr. Stark brings into play while working with children is the presence of her dog Gregory. Through the years, many kids and teenagers have attested to how their therapy sessions with Dr. Stark were facilitated simply by the fact that former therapy dogs Jimmy and Rita were present there! Now that Gregory is the new therapy dog, they'll feel the same way about him.

In addition to Whole Heart for Young Women, Dr. Stark is the author of Whole Heart for Girls plus the illustrated children's books The Fairy Godmother Next Door and The Fairy Godmother Babysits.

She also facilitates workshops on self-esteem, bullying, and empathy for children 6-18.

For more information: www.dramystark.com

Made in the USA
Middletown, DE
18 September 2019